How To Manage Money

The Influence Of Psychology On The Formation Of Our Financial Mindset

(An Assortment Of Financial Advice For Couples To Effectively Manage Their Finances)

George Duchesne

TABLE OF CONTENT

Introduction 1

Maintain Your Attention Directed Towards Your Objectives. 21

The Psychological Aspects Of Consumer Behavior 41

Improve Your Financial Literacy 65

Utilizing Your Credit Report As A Foundation For Strategic Planning 81

Acquire Knowledge On Unlocking Passive Income Strategies That Have The Potential To Transform Your Future 126

Introduction

I would like to express my gratitude and extend my congratulations to you for acquiring and downloading the book, titled "Enhancing the financial well-being of your funds."

This literary composition encompasses verified procedures and tactics to enhance the state of one's financial circumstances. This book will explore numerous practical approaches to effectively managing your finances, maintaining your budget, and ensuring your financial stability in the long term.

Although money may not provide solutions to all inquiries, it remains significant to possess an ample amount. Despite the often negative connotations associated with the concepts of money and wealth, they are indispensable for achieving personal liberation. However, the majority of individuals are inherently inclined to hold an opposing viewpoint. People generally avoid discussing financial matters or appearing overly motivated by money. None of us desire to appear excessively focused on financial gain. Consequently, we engage in minimal discourse, inquiries, or education regarding financial matters. Indeed, we acquire minimal or negligible insights regarding financial matters from our parents or educational institutions throughout our formative years. Even within the confines of academia, the subject of finances is rarely expounded upon by instructors unless one pursues a specialization in Finance. Consequently, how can one be expected to possess the requisite understanding of pivotal intricacies essential for cultivating a fiscally sound future? This presents a valuable opportunity for you to acquire knowledge about financial matters that were not previously provided to you. If you possess an unwavering resolve to enhance your financial condition, I encourage you to proceed and uncover the profound insights on effectively managing your finances to attain complete financial independence.

Thank you once again for your download of this book. I sincerely hope that you derive pleasure from it.

Copyright 2015 by Limitless North - All rights are reserved.

This document is intended to offer precise and trustworthy information pertaining to the subject and matter at hand. The publication is marketed under the premise that the publisher is not obligated to provide accounting or any other form of authorized or professional services. If guidance is needed, particularly of a legal or professional nature, it is advisable to engage the services of an experienced individual in the respective field.

- As per an endorsed and mutually accepted Declaration of Principles by both the Committee of the American Bar Association and the Committee of Publishers and Associations.

It is strictly prohibited to reproduce, duplicate, or transmit any portion of this document, whether through electronic methods or in a physical printed form. Unauthorized reproduction of this publication is strictly prohibited and any retention of this document is prohibited without prior written consent from the publisher. All rights reserved.

The information presented herein is declared to be accurate and cohesive. As such, any potential liability arising from negligence or any other form of non-compliance with the policies, procedures, or instructions provided herein is solely and entirely the responsibility of the recipient reader.

The publisher shall not bear any legal responsibility or liability for any compensation, damages, or monetary loss resulting from the information provided herein, whether directly or indirectly, under any circumstances.

The copyrights, excluding those held by the publisher, are exclusively owned by the respective authors.

The information provided here is strictly intended for informational purposes and is universally applicable. The presentation of the information is devoid of any contractual obligations or assurances of a guarantee.

The trademarks being utilized are being used without consent, and the publication of said trademarks is being conducted without authorization or endorsement from the trademark owner. The trademarks and brands mentioned in this book are solely provided for illustrative purposes and are the intellectual property of their respective owners. This document is in no way affiliated with or endorsed by these owners.

Prior to availing oneself of student loans

Those individuals who have not yet acquired educational loans should carefully consider several significant factors. This is a verdict of twenty-two.

that has the potential to exert a lasting influence on your life spanning several decades. Presented below are several recommendations for individuals considering student loans.

Take every possible measure to refrain from it.

If it is at all feasible, refrain from acquiring student loans. Seek out scholarships, explore opportunities for part-time employment, apply for work-study placements, or alternatively, inquire with your parents if they are able to provide assistance.

All possible alternatives must be meticulously examined before making the decision to accept a loan. If it is not necessary, refrain from acquisition.

Accept only what you need

The allure to acquire excessive loan amounts is quite compelling, particularly given that educational institutions often offer significantly more funding than necessary for essential expenses.

In the event that you find it absolutely necessary to utilize student loans for the purpose of financing your tertiary education, it is advised to solely accept the minimum sum that is required.

Government or private sector loans.

There are two categories of loans that are currently accessible, namely Federal and Private.

Federal loans are financed by the government, in this case, the United States.

The Department of Education administers federal loans, while private loans are originated by diverse entities including banks, credit unions, third-party organizations, state agencies, or the institution itself.

Federal Student Loans

Federal loans possess numerous advantages which render them more favorable in comparison to private loans. To begin with, it is customary for fixed interest rates to be offered alongside adaptable repayment alternatives. Another 23

An advantage of Federal loans is that repayment is not required until post-graduation, upon leaving educational institutions, or upon changing enrollment status to less than full time. The interest rate typically exhibits a lower magnitude than that of private loans, and hinges upon whether it is subsidized or unsubsidized. Furthermore, it is plausible for the interest to be deferred until your graduation.

Private loans necessitate a cosigner, whereas federal loans typically do not impose such a requirement. It is also plausible that the deduction of the interest rate on a federal loan is feasible; however, it should be noted that such deduction is not assured for private loans.

In conclusion, federal loans offer repayment options that are significantly more favorable in comparison to those for private loans. Consolidation of federal loans into a Direct Consolidation Loan is a viable option, whereas private loans may not always be eligible for this form of consolidation. Additionally, in the event that you encounter challenges in meeting your financial obligations following your completion of studies, it may be possible for you to defer or potentially reduce the amount you are required to repay. Federal loans do not incur any fees for early repayment, and it is possible for you to qualify for loan forgiveness for a portion of your loan amount. This is seldom the scenario for private loans.

In general, if there is an absolute necessity for obtaining a loan, it is advisable to opt for federal loans while ardently avoiding private loans. If you find yourself limited to relying on private loans, it is vital to acquire a comprehensive understanding of the terms and conditions associated with them. Engage in a thorough conversation regarding the repayment plans with the loan provider, and undertake diligent research to evaluate and compare multiple lenders prior to finalizing a decision.

Subsidized vs Unsubsidized

Subsidized loans are more preferable due to their superior terms.

These resources can be accessed by undergraduate students who have received financial assistance at any time, day or night.

The requirements and quantity are established by your educational institution. One notable advantage of these loans is that the Department of Education assumes responsibility for covering the loan interest, provided that the borrower maintains at least half-time enrollment in school. This interest coverage extends to the initial six-month period after the borrower's departure from school, commonly referred to as the grace period, as well as during any deferment periods experienced by the borrower.

Unsubsidized loans can be accessed by both graduate and undergraduate students, without the requirement of showcasing a financial need. Unlike the subsidized loan, one is obligated to remit the interest payments throughout all periods.

In summary, it is advisable to opt for a subsidized loan when presented with the choice between the two. For individuals who possess an unsubsidized loan, an effective approach would involve settling the accrued interest during their enrollment period. By adopting this method, they would solely be accountable for the principal amount upon completion of their studies, along with subsequent interest charges henceforth.

By opting for student loan refinancing, one can effectively reduce their interest rate and merge multiple loans together – a prudent approach that can lead to significant cost savings.

Consolidation essentially entails the amalgamation of multiple debts into a single sum, thereby enabling individuals to make payments towards a unified source rather than dispersing payments to three disparate sources.

When contemplating the option of refinancing, it is advisable to take into account both the prevailing interest rate as well as the duration of the loan.

The interest rate can potentially fluctuate or remain constant. A fixed interest rate remains constant over the duration of the loan, whereas a 25-year adjustable interest rate may fluctuate based on market conditions.

The variable rate fluctuates in accordance with economic variables.

When selecting an interest rate, it is not solely a matter of opting for the lowest one, although this aspect does contribute to the overall calculation.

Instead, it is crucial to select the option that aligns most effectively with your financial strategy.

If one does not anticipate an imminent increase in the interest rate, particularly within a span of approximately five years, opting for a variable interest rate might be more advantageous. Nevertheless, in the event that your loan duration extends to 15 or 20 years,

Over the course of several years, a consistent rate is the more desirable option. Furthermore, should you desire precise information regarding the exact payment amount for each occurrence, it would be more advisable to opt for a fixed rate.

The loan duration incorporates a higher degree of complexity; however, as a general principle, the shorter the loan duration, the greater the monthly installment, and conversely. When evaluating the duration of the loan, it is prudent to take into account the prevailing interest rate. In the event of a protracted loan term, it would be advisable to opt for the alternative showcasing a comparatively lower interest rate.

When engaging in dialogue regarding these choices with your lender, ensure that you select an option in which they can provide diligent guidance throughout the entirety of the process. It is crucial that you do not experience any sense of urgency or bewilderment at any stage of the proceedings. Attempt to engage in negotiations by utilizing your understanding of alternative lenders. It is important to exercise thorough research and evaluation to select the most suitable lender for your needs; it is crucial to avoid hasty decision-making in this matter.

Maintain Your Attention Directed Towards Your Objectives.

Why do it?

An imperative facet of the human condition is establishing objectives for our desired endeavors and diligently pursuing them. Despite the potential lack of directness or simplicity in the path towards our aspirations, the presence of life goals, regardless of their magnitude, is imperative for a contented livelihood. The overall well-being of individuals is enhanced by this phenomenon as it provides a sense of significance and direction, whilst also evoking curiosity.

Almost two millennia ago, Aristotle astutely noted, "A good start is equivalent to accomplishing half of the task." Regarding objectives, he is accurate (considering his frequent accuracy on various matters). By meticulously considering the establishment of our objectives, we enhance the likelihood of accomplishing them, thereby improving our self-appraisal and overall satisfaction with our lives.

Where to begin

- Decide. Take into account a desired objective or course of action that you wish to undertake. No matter the nature of the task at hand, so long as it aligns with your desires and ideally piques your interest or elicits excitement, it bears no significance. It is imperative that one harbors the ambition to achieve it for one's own benefit, instead of being driven by external factors or influences. Regardless of size, there are instances when commencing with smaller endeavors is simply preferable. Ambitious goals can serve as a source of inspiration, hence it is often beneficial if they slightly exceed one's current abilities.

• Please document it in written form. • Kindly express it in a written format. • I would appreciate if you could provide written documentation. • I request that you transfer the information into written form. • It is expected that you put the information in writing. • I kindly ask that you record it in written communication. Carefully. The probability of attaining our objectives is heightened when we formally document them. Establish a specific timeframe and delineate the criteria by which the attainment of your objectives will be determined in written form. What visual appearance will it possess, and what emotions will you experience upon its accomplishment? To whom or what does it pertain, that holds significance in your life? Rather than expressing a general desire for gardening, it is advisable to articulate your objective in a specific and time-bound manner. For instance, instead of stating, "I want to do some gardening," elaborate on your intentions by specifying the exact task and timeframe. An appropriate rephrasing could be, "My aim is to cultivate lettuces, carrots, and peas in the vacant area of my garden, ensuring completion by the conclusion of May." When formulating your goals, it is crucial to emphasize your desired outcomes, rather than focusing on what you wish to avoid. Instead of expressing the desire to no longer be overweight by saying, "I don't want to be overweight anymore," an alternative could be articulated as, "I aspire to regain the ability to comfortably adorn my preferred trousers once more."

- Inform someone. Furthermore, it appears that our chances of adhering to our objectives are enhanced when we disclose them to acquaintances.

- Dissect your objective. This holds significant importance, especially for individuals driven by lofty aspirations. Take into account the smaller goals that will contribute to the achievement of your primary objective. The pursuit of enhanced well-being through improved fitness and overall health stands as a notable objective, albeit one that may occasionally lack clarity. We can enhance precision by implementing a divisional approach. Hence, it may be more feasible to set a more attainable goal such as "engage in regular running sessions" or "successfully complete a non-stop run around the park within 20 minutes." Document these smaller targets and consider assigning specific deadlines to them. We are prone to maintaining our broader objective with greater consistency when we establish multiple intermediary goals, as such an approach renders each task more manageable, fostering a sense of achievement throughout the process.

- Formulate an initial action plan. In accordance with a traditional Chinese adage, every expedition commences with an initial stride. Even if the objective of covering a distance of 1,000 miles on foot does not align with your ultimate goal, mapping out and initiating your initial stride will prove advantageous in initiating progress. There is no justification, despite a lack of understanding of where to initiate. An initial course of action may encompass conducting online research on the topic of interest, identifying potential interviewees, or procuring relevant literature from the library. Additionally, contemplate your following course of action...and successive steps...

- Carry on. Occasionally, the pursuit of our objectives can present us with difficulties and frustrations; nevertheless, it is imperative that we persevere. Should you find that your current course of action is providing insufficient progress, consider exploring alternative steps that may yield more promising outcomes. If you are encountering difficulties, we suggest seeking counsel from your companions and associates. They could provide assistance in altering your outlook. It enhances the likelihood of our success if we contemplate multiple approaches in attaining our goals. In the event that you are genuinely disheartened, it would be advisable to momentarily cease your activities, reconsider, and subsequently revisit the initial objective you had documented. If necessary, feel free to modify your objective. Subsequently, I would suggest devoting additional consideration to the ensuing course of action.

- Celebrate. Upon achieving success, it is important to allocate a moment for celebration and express gratitude towards those individuals who provided their assistance. Reflect upon the various insights gained and valued throughout the course of your expedition. What upcoming projects or objectives do you have planned?

HABITS TO DEVELOP

The idea posits that individuals with substantial wealth reside in regions characterized by plentiful resources, enabling them to bask in heightened accomplishments and self-assuredness. If your aspiration is to amass a million-dollar fortune and achieve your objective, it is imperative to adhere to a set of principles that will facilitate the cultivation of the appropriate habits. When one's habits undergo transformation and conducive behaviors are cultivated, their accomplishments surpass anticipated outcomes.

However, what actions must one undertake in order to cultivate these behaviors?

Ensure that your goals are always prioritized

If your aspirations do not consistently reside within your heart or occupy your thoughts, you will undeniably struggle to achieve them. In the event that your aspirations entail the attainment of a desired vocation, financial growth, or perhaps another objective, and such aspirations occupy a limited space in your thoughts, how can they be effectively realized given the infrequency with which they are contemplated? Developing a novel routine typically requires a duration of approximately two months. Once your objectives are in your thoughts, promptly document them and position them in a visible and easily assessable location.

Develop a propensity for ongoing knowledge acquisition.

It is a common occurrence for individuals to neglect the reality that the world consistently presents them with the chance to acquire knowledge and embark on novel endeavors. When striving for success, it is imperative to enhance one's skills and elevate one's performance. Acquiring the ability to adapt to ongoing changes can help you realize that your previous customs were not yielding the desired outcomes you sought after. Irrespective of the modest extent of the skills one acquires, they possess the capacity to augment one's personal worth. Do not underestimate the potency of perpetual learning.

Acquire proficiency in the field of networking

Without effective networking, it is not feasible to achieve your desired aspirations. The manner in which you carry yourself holds significant importance. If you were to deliver a presentation on your business, dreams, or passion, it is imperative that you exhibit confidence and assertiveness. This will leave a lasting impression on your audience. Networking provides opportunities for you to connect with individuals who possess similar values and passions as yourself.

Develop the skill of exhibiting patience

Occasionally, one may experience a sense of irritation and frustration when their diligent efforts fail to produce the intended results. Nonetheless, it is imperative to not allow such setbacks to dampen one's spirits or undermine their dedication towards pursuing their aspirations. It is a widely acknowledged truth that significant accomplishments typically require time and perseverance, as evidenced by the proverbial saying that Rome was not built in a day. It is acceptable if your intended objectives are not achieved within the specified timeframe; it is important to bear in mind that noteworthy accomplishments often require a considerable duration to become firmly established.

Make sure not to neglect the importance of adequate sleep.

In order to foster productivity and ensure the execution of one's work to the utmost level of excellence, obtaining a sufficient amount of quality sleep is imperative. Although your schedule may frequently be filled to capacity, obtaining adequate rest enables rejuvenation of both mind and body. As a consequence of an extensive agenda, one might be inclined to forego sleep in order to fulfill commitments; however, this typically proves to be ineffectual. One additional period subtracted from your designated resting time has the potential to induce fatigue and hinder overall productivity. After you have sufficiently rested, your body and mind will be more inclined and prepared to commence your day.

▪ Embrace mistakes as they arise

During the process of personal and professional advancement, one is likely to encounter inevitable errors, which cannot be entirely circumvented, but rather present opportunities for acquiring new insights and knowledge. It is important to note that errors may arise due to negligence or inadequate planning, yet these can still be prevented. Mistakes and errors afford individuals and groups a valuable opportunity to self-assess and explore, thus facilitating the acquisition of new competencies and proficiencies for future endeavors. Engulfing oneself in sorrow and regret due to one's mistakes provides no viable solution. Instead, it is imperative to reflect upon these errors and discern avenues for improvement in subsequent endeavors.

There should be ample opportunity for expansion.

The inclusion of opportunities for both professional and personal development is of paramount importance in the pursuit of one's aspirations. Maintaining an open-minded and growth-oriented mindset throughout your journey towards success is paramount, as it serves as a constant reminder of your humble beginnings. It is advisable to exert conscious effort in assessing your progress, particularly when working towards long-term objectives. This approach will enhance your effectiveness and provide a sense of fulfillment. Should you find yourself experiencing a sense of being fully consumed or overburdened, it is advisable to break down your objectives into more manageable segments, thereby diminishing the weight and complexity of the workload. Maturation necessitates a substantial investment of time and a diligent execution of effort.

Attempt to refrain from providing justifications for your actions.

Providing justifications for oneself will impede the progress of one's endeavors. In the presence of an obstacle, endeavor to identify and implement solutions to effectively address the given challenge, instead of attributing your shortcomings to external factors. You are presented with the privileged opportunity to collaborate with your mentor, leveraging their expertise to facilitate the identification of potential challenges. Do not allow excuses to exert undue influence over you.

While ascending the path to success, it is crucial to maintain a humble and courteous demeanor.

As you ascend the path towards success, endeavor to maintain a high level of respectfulness. Upon the successful accomplishment of your goals, you will experience a profound sense of gratification derived from your adherence to the principles of respect towards those who aided you throughout your journey towards triumph.

The Psychological Aspects Of Consumer Behavior

Purchasing items not only entails a mere monetary transaction within a retail setting, but rather encompasses profound psychological ramifications. Large corporations utilize scientific research studies as a tool to promote and market their products. Frequently, these instances entail psychological tactics employed to compel consumers to select their product over that of their competitors.

This endeavor encompasses not only the development of a prosperous advertising campaign but also the implementation of highly defined psychological methodologies.

In order to adhere to your budgetary constraints, you must acquire the knowledge required to identify and discern these manipulation techniques, thus becoming familiar with their tactics.

To begin with, observe the arrangement of the items within the supermarket premises. All the products that have been advertised are strategically positioned in the foremost display area, ensuring their prominent visibility to rapidly capture attention and stimulate consumer engagement. Items that are more affordable or have not been promoted are positioned higher or lower on the shelf, ensuring they do not receive immediate visibility and thus have a reduced chance of being sold.

The music played in supermarkets serves an essential purpose, namely that of fostering a positive atmosphere (consisting of commercially oriented, upbeat songs) and motivating customers to engage in purchasing activities. In the supermarket you will never find rock songs or melancholy tracks, but only the latest commercial hits and the most transmitted radio songs.

Indeed, the presence of a melancholic tune in no manner hinders the act of purchasing a pack of biscuits, correct?

Yet another effective approach to stimulate the purchase is through competitive pricing.

Frequently, the value of a merchandise is intentionally raised and subsequently reduced to its actual price, thereby generating a "discount" that serves as an incentive for consumers to make a purchase. However, in reality, this is merely a strategic presentation designed to create the appearance of being more cost-effective compared to the competition.

I would like to provide an instance that serves to enhance comprehension of this concept (an episode I personally observed).

A computer system vendor engages in a customer interview to present and utilizes a psychological strategy in order to market their product.

The cost of the product is one hundred dollars. The seller presents the $200 product to the customer, who expresses their interest but deems the price to be excessive. The vendor proceeds to feign an attempt at providing an exclusive discount "solely for your benefit" and suggests a revised price of $100 for the product. A reduction of 50%, a truly advantageous offer that presents conditions difficult to refuse.

The consumer makes a purchase under the assumption of being afforded special privileges and having secured the most advantageous transaction of their professional life. However, the reality is that the consumer has been deceived, or at the very least, misled into believing in a discounted offer that lacks veracity.

This deception carries numerous inherent hazards, as it is only a matter of time until someone detects the fraudulent scheme. However, if the vendor or establishment experiences a high influx of customers, they stand a significant chance of selling a substantial quantity of items before their misdeeds are exposed.

Consider the sales season in retail establishments; a significant number of fraudulent practices occur whereby merchants advertise exorbitant discounts (60/70%) while maintaining the original price.

By utilizing online resources and dedicated platforms that provide price comparisons, individuals can endeavor to circumvent these fraudulent schemes.

An additional pricing strategy involves offering various pricing options (each with distinct features) to enhance the appeal of the product, particularly the one that falls in the middle.

A quick example.

A symposium offering various bundled options.

The initial package is priced at $100, encompassing a snapshot alongside the guest, an autograph, a premium seat in the front row, and a delectable brunch. It seems very convenient.

The second package is priced at $300 and encompasses identical features as the first package, accompanied by an exclusive 10-minute interview with the guest and a commemorative photograph accompanied by a personalized dedication. A sum of $300 represents a significant amount of money, thus deterring a majority of individuals from purchasing this package due to the notable disparity in price and the meager additional features it presents.

However, it is possible to enhance the appeal and attractiveness of this package by introducing an additional tier with a higher price.

This package constitutes the third option available, priced at $500, encompassing the entire range of services previously extended, along with the inclusion of a personalized video call with the esteemed guest and a shirt bearing their autograph. Due to the implementation of this strategy, the $300 package has acquired a highly competitive edge, resulting in increased purchases by a larger consumer base. By incorporating an additional package worth $750, the $500 package will acquire a competitive edge.

This psychological technique is highly beneficial given its ability to enhance the desirability of a product priced at $300. Upon careful reflection, we come to acknowledge that $300 constitutes a substantial amount of money. Furthermore, it becomes evident that the package priced at $100 is indeed the most economical option. However, the deployment of a psychological manipulation compels us to perceive the $300 package as the superior choice.

Steve Jobs himself employed a comparable approach in revealing the introduction of the inaugural iPad model.

The Apple founder announced the technical features of the innovative product to the world while "$ 999" was written on a big screen.

The audience appeared to have a limited level of interest, as they found the product to be commendable and groundbreaking, yet expressed concerns about its pricing, which was deemed excessive. However, Jobs ingeniously disclosed that the product's commercial value was indeed "$999," but clarified that this figure did not represent the actual selling price.

Simultaneously, the displayed price underwent a transformation and depicted the value of "$499", instigating a tremendous burst of jubilation throughout the entire room. An exemplary demonstration of psychological manipulation, serving as a prime illustration of the initial tactic outlined.

$499 represents a significant amount, yet Steve Jobs has magnified this figure through his exceptional prowess.

These represent only a few of the tactics that are being diligently researched on a daily basis in an effort to promote and sell a product. It is imperative for us to familiarize ourselves with these methods (although they are not illicit, they can be bothersome) in order to avoid being deceived and succumbing to impulsive purchases that may disrupt our monthly financial plan.

Step 2: Acquire the Knowledge to Manage Your Finances and Strive for Economic Independence

Effectively managing your finances involves developing and implementing a comprehensive strategy that effectively allocates your income towards prioritized expenditures aligned with your overarching financial goals and overall well-being. Due to its efficacy in this pursuit, a comprehensive financial plan typically takes the form of a well-constructed budget.

A budget is an indispensable financial management instrument that one should not overlook. The primary objective of this tool is to assist you in assuming command of your finances by enabling you to strategize the allocation of your net income in light of your financial obligations and objectives. As a financial planning instrument, a budget enables one to attain a comprehensive understanding of their expenditure patterns, thus recognizing the impact of these patterns on their overall financial well-being.

In cases where one is residing beyond their financial capabilities, by exceeding their earnings or income, implementing a budget enables the identification of specific areas where one can make financial adjustments that promote increased financial flexibility and room for maneuver.

As an illustration, in the event that you are exceeding your financial capabilities, a budget serves as a mechanism enabling you to identify that a total of $1,000 is spent on recreational activities. Furthermore, this instrument empowers you to discern that through reducing your expenditures on leisure activities by fifty percent, you can effectively liberate a sum of $500. This sum can subsequently be allocated towards the settlement of debts, thereby augmenting your overall financial standing, as well as towards savings or any other commendable endeavor, be it acquiring essential items, establishing an emergency fund, initiating an online venture, nurturing personal growth, and the like.

Developing a budget entails a fairly straightforward procedure, yet it is indispensable in crafting an effective financial management strategy tailored to your specific needs. To establish a comprehensive strategy for budgeting, managing finances, and attaining financial independence: "

Record all sources of income

If you have completed the initial action step, you are already aware of your net income(s), as we mentioned that this information could be ascertained by reviewing your bank statement or net pay slip.

Calculate the difference between your expenses and your income by subtraction.

Once more, after thoroughly assimilating the fundamental principles conveyed in the initial phase and successfully carrying out the initial actionable step, you should possess a comprehensive understanding of your monthly expenditures and all the payments you incur on a monthly basis.

As previously noted, you can ascertain your monthly expenses by examining your bank statement from one month to the next. Alternatively, if you predominantly make cash payments, you can manually monitor and document each occurrence of spending within a designated payment cycle.

Additionally, I would like to suggest that you take an extra measure by categorizing your expenses into two distinct groups: fixed and variable, as well as needs and wants.

Fixed expenses encompass any financial outlays that demonstrate a consistent pattern from month to month. Illustrative instances include rent, mortgage payments, obligatory debt and loan installments, internet charges, and other comparable fixed expenses. The majority of the expenditures within this category constitute a significant portion of your monthly financial obligations, which encompass the essential amount of money required to successfully navigate from one month to the next.

Fluctuating expenses exhibit monthly variation and commonly consist of essential components such as allocation for groceries, expenditures on cable, internet, or recreational activities, dining out, fuel or transportation costs, and similar expenditures.

PLEASE NOTE: It is important to emphasize that effective financial management entails maintaining a lifestyle that is below one's means or earning a surplus income each month. This surplus can then be allocated towards savings, debt reduction, investment, and ultimately, attaining financial independence.

If the calculation reveals that your expenditures surpass your net income, you are facing a financial predicament that necessitates crucial financial decisions and sacrifices. In order to attain financial liberty and tranquility, it is imperative that you take control of your finances and cease worrying about the payment of bill X or the fulfillment of financial demand Y.

Please make the necessary adjustments as deemed appropriate.

In order to effectively utilize a budget as an effective instrument for managing your finances and advancing towards achieving financial independence, it is essential to adapt and modify it based on your existing financial circumstances and objectives.

In the event that an assessment of your financial situation indicates that your spending exceeds your income, and given that your present financial objective is to reduce debt or accumulate funds for a business venture or emergency fund, it would be prudent to primarily focus on your variable expenses and implement alterations or sacrifices that align with this financial objective.

A budget ought to possess adaptability and be tailored to meet individual financial requirements and objectives. It is imperative for it to facilitate the fulfillment of all your financial obligations within a specified payment cycle, while also enabling the allocation of surplus funds towards debt settlement and purposeful saving activities, such as establishing an emergency fund.

Please be advised that while it is within our capacity to discuss specific budgeting percentages and suggest a definitive budgetary allocation, such an approach wouldn't align with the intent of this guide, which aims to assist you in developing a personalized and effective financial management strategy.

Therefore, rather than instructing you to adhere to the widely accepted 50/30/20 budgeting principle which suggests allocating 50% of your net income towards necessary expenses, 30% towards discretionary spending, and 20% towards debt repayment and savings, this manual encourages evaluating your present financial situation and objectives, and subsequently adjusting these proportions as necessary.

Having taken that into account, it is imperative to include saving and debt repayment as fundamental components of your monthly budget allocations. By consistently repaying debt, you can effectively enhance your credit rating and improve your overall financial situation. This is because carrying debt hinders the attainment of financial freedom. Additionally, by saving instead of relying on loans, you reduce your dependency on debt and expedite progress towards your individual financial objectives.

The determination of the proportion of your income allocated towards savings and debt settlements is entirely at your discretion, contingent upon both your present financial circumstances and long-term financial objectives. Consequently, there exists no obligatory regulation mandating a 10% savings rate; rather, the amount you choose to save is at your discretion, contingent upon your financial circumstances and objectives.

An exploration of debt repayment strategies and attaining financial independence

Incurring debt will burden you and protract your path towards achieving financial independence. It is imperative for you to exert utmost diligence in ensuring the consistent repayment of your debts.

Continuously allocate the minimum payment towards all of your outstanding debts, and enhance your financial approach by prioritizing additional funds or the surplus obtained through financial compromises towards the repayment of a specific debt. This could involve focusing on the smallest debt or the debt with the highest interest rate. The greater your commitment is to consistently servicing your debts, the stronger command you will exercise over your financial matters, leading you progressively closer to achieving ultimate financial independence.

Action step

Employ the aforementioned tactics to develop a versatile budget that is tailored to your needs and enables you to accumulate savings towards your financial objectives and ultimate financial independence.

Improve Your Financial Literacy

Money related proficiency, as delineated, refers to the acquisition of education or knowledge pertaining to adeptly managing personal funds. This encompasses the aspects of strategic planning, financial contribution, retirement preparation, and even tax assessment strategizing.

Perhaps, a significant number of us are aware of how to create a monthly budget. However, it should be noted that planning constitutes merely a single aspect of financial management. By improving your financial literacy, you will be able to increase your income and generate greater profits.

Begin Now

There is always potential for further enhancement in one's understanding of financial matters. Enhance your understanding of topics such as philanthropy, estate planning, social security benefits, credit card mechanisms, long-term financial planning, government social security programs, real estate investment, insurance policies, retirement planning, and taxation. Address a single topic at a time. Commence with the subject that resonates with you most and proceed to construct a solid foundation of financial knowledge.

Offer monetary assessments

Financial evaluations can serve as exceptional educational tools for employees at large. Typically, an evaluation provides an illustration of the individual's fiscal strengths and areas of concern. It fosters engagement with employees and provides a solid foundation for financial goal setting.

Typically, individuals experience uneasiness regarding their finances due to uncertainty about the sources of pressure they are facing. An evaluation can assist in uncovering these reasons while also significantly alleviating the concerns of representatives, aiding in their understanding of where they should prioritize their efforts and investments. It is akin to completing a comprehensive risk assessment aimed at evaluating one's overall well-being. In some instances, the financial assessment can serve as a catalyst for taking measures to enhance one's fiscal stability. For example, an individual with limited financial flexibility may exhibit a disproportionate focus on retirement planning rather than actively managing their existing debt.

Begin an Investment Club

The purpose behind establishing a venture club is to gain knowledge about investing in stocks and generate profitable returns on investments. This is an extensive commitment for a group of ten to fifteen individuals who seek to enhance their knowledge of the stock market by investing in stocks. The National Association of Investors Corporation is a non-profit organization that provides education on speculation and valuable investment experience through investment clubs.

Track your records continuously

Many entrepreneurs tend to prioritize organizing their books only once a year, specifically during the tax season, due to being overwhelmed by other business demands. The current accounting software, such as Quickbooks, simplifies the process of synchronizing financial transactions in real time, alleviating much of the labor involved in maintaining accurate records. Take advantage of the diverse range of reporting options available to provide accurate descriptions of your company's financials. - As stated by Ismael Wrixen of FE International - According to Ismael Wrixen, the CEO of FE International -

Ismael Wrixen, the representative from FE International, expressed - Ismael Wrixen from FE International mentioned

Utilize information total applications

Employ a complimentary comprehensive information platform that enables you to assess your financial well-being, including elements such as cash flow, credit, and more. Individuals engaged in entrepreneurial pursuits possess unique requirements, therefore it is advisable to employ an application specifically designed for small-scale enterprises. The distinguished individuals have successfully achieved a balanced integration of artificial intelligence to provide recommendations within an educational framework, enabling one to make more intelligent choices and acquire knowledge along the way. - Gregory Ott, Nav Incorporated

Employ online tools - In addition to the CNN article, there is a digital tool available that facilitates the calculation of the duration required to completely repay a specific sum of credit card debt. There are a plethora of online calculators similar to this one. Undoubtedly, Millionaire Mommy Next Door placed a substantial order for a comprehensive range of these tools. There is genuinely no need for you to recall the mathematical assumptions underlying these devices in order to make use of them. A significant proportion of these calculators will enhance your ability to strategically plan your financial objectives, as they provide a more precise estimate of your financial position.

Stalk individual finance sites

A growing multitude of websites, on-air personalities, and even the aforementioned personal finance experts have integrated social media into their campaign strategy. Emulate or draw inspiration from esteemed financial experts in order to acquire fresh insights on managing your finances in the present as well as in the future.

Moreover, by diligently monitoring the financial sections of news platforms on Facebook and Twitter, you can effectively stay abreast of the latest developments and comprehend their impacts on your personal finances. By staying cognizant of financial news stories, you can employ this knowledge in your everyday life.

Enroll in a complimentary web-based financial literacy course.

The internet serves as a loyal companion to you on your digital journey. There are several resources available to you, should you require the opportunity to flex your financial prowess as mentioned earlier.

Ultimately, financial literacy pertains to attaining autonomy, self-reliance, and tranquility. A life can be led without encountering predators such as sharks. It is typically accessed when individuals make prompt, well-informed decisions. In any event, in South Africa, there are 95 men for every 100 women that implies we women have more... um...

labor. It is within our control to alter the trajectory of African women.

Immerse yourself in the experience of a TED talk

TED talks originated as a discourse on progress within the realms of technology and science, yet they have subsequently expanded in scope to encompass a broader range of subjects, spanning from music to finance. Although attending a TED conference can impose a significant financial burden of $4,000 or higher per attendee, individuals with a keen interest in personal finance can explore engaging financial presentations on the official ted.com website.

This educational facility surpasses mere discussions on personal finance topics by providing a fresh perspective on conventional guidance. The insights presented at TED talks would be most advantageous for individuals who possess a high level of receptiveness to the fundamental principles of personal finance. However, those who are just embarking on their journey of financial planning may also find these ideas equally engrossing.

Irrespective of whether you incorporate these assets into your personal financial portfolio or consolidate them into a single entity, your enhanced financial proficiency will bring you closer to achieving significant fiscal advancement.

Conduct preliminary investigation into monetary items. You may not possess a substantial amount of disposable income, but that should not deter you from making efforts to comprehend the available alternatives. If you lack comprehension regarding the functionality of benefits, such as their relation to you and the financial markets, you can readily acquire information through online resources. Commence by focusing on the fundamental aspects, such as Individual Savings Accounts (ISAs), investment accounts, annuities, premium free credit, and similar entities. Make an earnest effort to attain a comprehensive understanding of how these components synergistically contribute to the establishment of immaculate financial stability.

Organize progression arranging

A crucial aspect of effectively managing your business also involves establishing a contingency or backup plan in the event of any unforeseen circumstances or the departure of your partner(s). Sitting down with a Certified Financial Planner (CFP®) can provide you with the opportunity to address these deficiencies in your business strategy. During this interim period, you can leverage the opportunity to collaborate with a Certified Financial Planner to seek guidance and enhance your financial literacy.

Explore opportunities for acquiring comprehensive expertise - As a valued customer of a financial institution or similar organization, you have the privilege to schedule appointments at your convenience and seek expert guidance. During my time in school, I initiated the establishment of a Vanguard Roth IRA based on the prudence imparted by my parents, as I had limited comprehension on several matters. Therefore, I called Vanguard's client benefit line frequently and asked inquiries concerning dollar cost averaging, subsidize sorts, and assign assets. The majority of the financial institutions' record delegates exhibit a high level of professionalism and expertise, making it decidedly favorable to receive explanations directly from knowledgeable individuals.

Know about the ruins. One of the key components of budgetary education is having the capacity to comprehend monetary difficulties and how to react to them without exacerbating them. There are always risks associated with any financial domain; however, having a comprehensive understanding of the consequences of failing to comply with the terms of a debt agreement or the dynamics of interest rates, both advantageous and detrimental, will enable you to make well-informed decisions that will significantly influence your financial situation in a positive manner. There is a substantial amount of data available on the internet and through organizations such as moneyadviceservice.org.uk.

Save 10% of salary

It is imperative to practice financial conservation. Life is unpredictable, as unfortunate events such as the loss of a family member, involvement in a car accident, or sudden unemployment can occur. There exist numerous unforeseen circumstances that have the potential to immerse themselves into an individual's existence. It is consistently advisable to align oneself with prudence. It is important to acknowledge that the awareness of your ability to modify your habits empowers you to take control of your financial affairs.

Utilizing Your Credit Report As A Foundation For Strategic Planning

In the preceding chapter, we gained an understanding of the utmost significance that your payment history holds for the credit agencies responsible for assessing your credit score. As this credit score holds significant weight in determining forthcoming credit prospects, it is of utmost importance that you commence undertaking measures at present to rectify your credit standing. The initial step involves reflecting upon your payment history and deriving insight from previous errors.

We all make mistakes. Certain errors possess a higher level of financial consequence than others, though. It is crucial at present that you acknowledge these errors and initiate a course of action to address these concerns. Presumably, you possess a comprehensive understanding of all your areas of concern. It is imperative that you be cognizant of the exact individual or entity to whom you owe a debt. Now is the opportune moment to carefully arrange and organize all of those troublesome bills and collection notices. However, there exists a superior and more optimal approach to obtain this information. Rather than sifting through an abundance of envelopes or searching for buried electronic correspondences, we recommend requesting a complimentary copy of your credit report.

If you make a request, each of the aforementioned credit organizations is obligated to furnish you with an annual credit report at no cost. This is to facilitate the monitoring of your credit and enhance your level of consumer awareness. Do not concern yourself with the 10% impact on your credit score resulting from credit inquiries. As previously stated in the preceding chapter, the matter at hand does not pertain to sporadic inspections. However, frequent and compulsive credit report inquiries, whether initiated by yourself or by businesses or institutions with whom you are seeking to establish credit relationships, will have adverse effects on your creditworthiness, even if only to a minor extent.

Upon receiving your credit report, you will have access to a comprehensive overview of all credit accounts that may be associated with you. Kindly be advised that the operations of each credit agency may vary slightly. In the event that you establish a new line of credit and subsequently examine your credit report within a short timeframe, it is possible that the recent addition may not be immediately discernible. Recall the multitude of factors involved in determining your credit score. Indeed, that information will comprise your credit report. Contrary to its simplistic scoring approach, your credit report manifests as a comprehensive portrayal of your credit history and activity.

All of your lines of credit will be showcased. Each lender will provide a comprehensive listing of the number of accounts you hold with them, account balances, available credit, credit limits, debt to credit ratios, and monthly payment amounts associated with each account. The credit agencies have intentionally cultivated credit reports that are readily comprehensible to consumers, ensuring that the information imparted within them is inherently uncomplicated. This aspect of the credit-repair procedure is undeniably centered on self-awareness. Currently, our primary focus lies in identifying any lines of credit that are being disregarded or exhibiting an elevated debt to credit ratio.

A significant disparity between debt and credit can raise concerns among prospective lenders, particularly within specific credit categories. Lenders express apprehension over revolving loans displaying a substantial debt to credit ratio. Revolving credit refers to a form of credit characterized by the absence of predetermined and fixed repayment obligations. Contrast this with a loan obtained by a student or from a bank. The borrower of a bank loan is engaged in the utilization of installment credit. To clarify, if you were to borrow a sum of $1200, you would need to make monthly payments of $110 for a duration of 12 months in order to fully repay the principal amount of the loan, in addition to the accrued interest. On the other hand, revolving credit does not entail any predetermined payment obligations. Credit cards can be defined as a form of renewable credit. The monthly payment amount will be contingent upon the utilization of your credit line, in the event that a credit card company grants you a $500 line of credit. Ordinarily, revolving credit frequently entails significantly elevated interest rates. In brief, it becomes more challenging to settle the debt once a substantial financial liability has been amassed. Consequently, a substantial debt to credit ratio pertaining to revolving credit accounts can have adverse effects on your creditworthiness and create an unfavorable perception among lenders.

It is crucial to bear in mind that the credit bureaus will utilize the data contained in your credit report for the purpose of calculating your credit score. They will not make inquiries with your acquaintances or relatives to assess your credibility as a borrower. They will examine your report and develop a numerical rating. To the credit agencies, you represent a comprehensive record of your credit transactions with different lenders. Additionally, your credit score is likely to be the primary factor that a lender takes into account when evaluating your eligibility for a loan or line of credit. It is imperative that you assess your credit score and report with the perspective of a prospective creditor. This approach will serve to incentivize and inspire you towards fostering a more robust credit profile.

Chapter 3: Repayment Strategies

There exist two prevailing perspectives regarding strategies for addressing financial indebtedness. According to one academic perspective, it is recommended to commence by targeting the smallest debts initially, those with minimal repayment obligations and swift resolution periods. In this manner, you will effectively address the minor liabilities within a brief timeframe, thereby enabling you to focus on the substantial debts without the need to allocate financial resources to the smaller obligations. An alternative perspective suggests that one should not focus on the magnitude of the debts, but rather prioritize considering their interest rates. According to this model, prioritizing a debt of $2,500 bearing an interest rate of 23.8% is recommended over a student loan amounting to $36,000 with an interest rate of 3.8%.

Both perspectives possess their own strengths.

The initial perspective adopts an approach of dividing and conquering. The majority of its advantages primarily pertain to the realm of psychology. By directing your attention towards lesser debts, you will eventually end up with a reduced number of accounts. This strategy is advantageous due to the fact that, by reducing the number of accounts that require attention, you will eventually shift your focus towards the larger accounts that are more difficult to settle. Nevertheless, this approach exhibits a significant drawback. By prioritizing accounts with lower outstanding balances, it fails to take into account the potential interest gains on larger accounts that carry a higher interest rate. It is possible that the interest rates of your accounts with lower balances are comparatively lower.

As a consequence of prioritizing the repayment of these accounts, you may incur greater interest expenses associated with larger outstanding debts.

According to popular belief, Albert Einstein purportedly stated that compound interest is the most formidable force in the cosmos. Regardless of whether or not the renowned scientist actually expressed these words, it is indisputable that interest possesses significant influence. Interest possesses the ability to augment the sum of your indebtedness. Undoubtedly, the lending institutions generate their profits by means of interest, as it allows them to reap monetary gains from the funds they provide. Keeping this perspective in consideration, let us now ponder upon the advantages of the second ideology. The alternative perspective posits that the primary emphasis should be placed on settling debts with the highest interest rates. The advantages of this strategy should be readily apparent at this juncture. By directing our attention towards the debts possessing the highest interest rates, which are generally associated with revolving credit instruments such as credit cards, we can mitigate the amount of financial resources expended on interest charges throughout the duration of the loan repayment process. One drawback of this particular perspective is that it may necessitate a lengthier duration for the complete repayment of all outstanding debts. Debts bearing lower interest rates may persist for a greater duration while your attention is directed towards those debts carrying higher interest rates. This could potentially lead to you experiencing a sense of inadequate progress in reducing your debt.

Thus, may I inquire as to which strategy I should employ? This question does not possess a universal applicability. The response is contingent upon not solely the nature of your debts, but also on your individual characteristics. The determination of your debt management approach is influenced by factors such as your remuneration, standard of living, and obligations. As previously stated, both strategies possess their respective advantages. Although the advantages of the initial approach are primarily psychological, it is important not to overlook the advantages of being able to visually track your progress in effectively managing your debt. Observing a symmetrical debt decrease to a null amount can serve as a profound catalyst for enhancing self-assurance and providing the impetus requisite to maintain a steadfast course. Of utmost significance, it serves as a reminder that you are steadily advancing. Although the second perspective permits the accumulation of interest savings and mitigates the drawback of perpetually paying off a loan without progressing financially.

The optimal approach would probably entail incorporating elements from both strategies. If you are willing to forego expenditures of $50 per month on dining out, with the aim of swiftly resolving a minor balance over the course of a few months, while concurrently setting aside a sufficient sum each month to make substantial headway on a balance with high interest, you shall subsequently obtain advantages of both psychological and monetary nature. Irrespective of the approach you opt to employ, ensure that it is tailored to your needs. The foremost priority is to establish objectives for oneself and diligently pursue their attainment. Utilize the provided information to shape your judgment and adhere to it steadfastly.

Developing an Effective Financial Plan

Your purpose is not just to create a budget but to create a good one. The likelihood of accomplishing your objectives is heightened when you possess a well-calibrated budget. Could you please provide instructions on how to create one?

First step: Establish the purpose behind your actions

Prior to embarking on the budgeting process, it is imperative to ascertain the underlying rationale behind the need for a budget. Your objective should be to establish your financial priorities and achieve equilibrium between your expenditures and income. This straightforward procedure has the potential to facilitate the prompt settlement of outstanding debts, enhance financial planning for expenditures, and enable accumulation of funds for significant acquisitions or enjoyable vacations. It is imperative to establish attainable objectives concerning the desired outcomes you intend to achieve through budgeting. What is your desired vision for your financial situation one year from now? Having identified the key priorities, utilize this knowledge to formulate your financial objectives. For example:

Do not harbor any apprehension that this might be intricate, as it is truly not the case. One might consider establishing a near-term objective encompassing the repayment of a specific portion of one's financial obligations, the acquisition of a new household appliance, or the undertaking of a planned journey to a particular location. When establishing these objectives, it is important to adhere to the SMART framework, which emphasizes the principles of specificity, measurability, achievability, realism/relevance, and time sensitivity. Establishing clear objectives facilitates the efficient allocation of resources by ensuring that you have already determined and ranked your priorities. "You have the option to organize your objectives in the subsequent fashion:

Suggestion: It can be significantly more motivating to record the figures on a physical medium such as a sheet of paper. Therefore, you are welcome to jot down something of a similar nature.

Second Step: Monitoring Your Daily Expenditures and Earnings

Upon attaining a comprehensive comprehension of your financial objectives, it is now opportune to ascertain the precise allocation of funds. We possess distinctive spending habits. Certain habits may have a positive impact, whereas others may be the root cause of our perpetual financial challenges.

The minor expenditures that we allocate our finances towards are ultimately what contribute to the overall expenses. Please be mindful of the minute sums of money that you expend on a daily basis. Familiarize yourself with the total amount they accumulate by day's end. This can be achieved through the establishment of a meticulous spending journal, a concise compilation where each and every expenditure, no matter how minuscule, is meticulously recorded to the exact dollar. Here is where you will acquire insights into your expenditure patterns. This exemplifies the practice commonly known as monitoring one's expenditures. Commence by selecting the desired duration for monitoring expenditures; typically, one week is considered the minimum timeframe.

The same principle applies to your income. Please document each and every source of income you receive, including but not limited to your business profits, child tax benefits, commissions, and wages. Please record any recurring funds you receive. This task could be relatively simple as, in numerous cases, our sources of revenue are transparent, leaving no ambiguity regarding the knowledge of one's earnings.

Please be advised that it is not advisable to monitor your expenses based on what you believe is appropriate. Alternatively, monitor your true expenditures and earnings.

What method or tool do you utilize for tracking purposes? Here are several suggestions:

Utilizing a Notebook and a Pen: This time-tested approach remains effective. It can be utilized to effortlessly monitor every item. Each expense item category can be recorded on its own dedicated page, allowing for ample space to add notes for each individual expense item. One could alternatively print budgeting templates, such as those available in PDF format, and proceed to complete them in their entirety. Enclosed herewith is a comprehensive monthly expense file, which is intended to provide you with a thorough understanding of the process at hand.

Spreadsheets

This is among the most straightforward if you possess a basic understanding of computers. One advantageous aspect of this particular option is the abundance of downloadable templates available. This eliminates the need to create a document from scratch as you can simply fill in the relevant information in a satisfactory manner.

Financial Software

One may opt to utilize Mint.com or alternative software options for the purpose of monitoring and managing their expenditures.

Ultimately, assess and contrast your earnings and expenditures in order to determine the resulting surplus or shortfall. There will be instances in which your expenditure surpasses your earnings, potentially due to factors such as receiving a tax refund, accumulating credit card debt, and other similar circumstances. If you are dissatisfied with the inexplicable vanishing of your funds and weary of constantly deferring your financial aspirations, the present moment presents an opportune occasion to proactively assume control over your finances, rather than being controlled by them.

Utilize the data gathered from the expense tracker that you have diligently maintained to analyze your spending patterns, subsequently discerning the underlying motivations behind your expenditures on specific items. I will proceed to delineate certain behaviors and subsequently provide a brief overview of strategies for managing them.

Buying name brands

Certainly, it is understandable that one may perceive themselves as a devoted patron of a particular brand. However, have you contemplated the possibility of procuring generic or pre-owned items? You may ascertain that they possess an equal level of proficiency. Do not allow your personal prejudices to influence your financial decisions.

Impulse buying

In the event that you discover yourself making unplanned purchases, you can alternatively establish a predetermined allocation for personal expenses, permitting you to allocate funds for discretionary purchases. If you genuinely desire the system to be effective, kindly incorporate this into your envelope system. Furthermore, it is advisable to refrain from carrying any additional currency or credit cards while venturing out in search of items. One may potentially engage in impulsive purchasing without thoroughly considering the implications.

You are not aware of the allocation of your funds.

Now you have a clear understanding of precisely where your funds are allocated. Keep tracking it.

Exhausting all funds without practicing fiscal restraint.

This undesirable behavior can be rectified by implementing a direct deposit system for your savings.

Step three entails the identification of priorities.

During the duration of approximately one month, you have diligently monitored and recorded your financial outlays and expenses. Once you have comprehended the precise amount you expend on each individual item, you can initiate the process of eliminating the items that are not essential for your livelihood. Obviously, there will be items that you've been spending on throughout the tracking period that you really shouldn't have been spending on. Identify and articulate your desires and requirements. Needs encompass essential elements for sustenance such as nourishment and shelter, whereas wants pertain to non-essential items or desires that are not vital for survival. It is necessary for you to classify your expenditures into essential requirements and non-essential desires. The purpose of this is to assist you in distinguishing between what you should discard and what you ought to retain.

You may come to realize that you consume an excessive amount of coffee or engage in extravagant spending, thus necessitating a reduction in these habits.

Please be advised that budgeting entails being deliberate in allocating funds for both expenditures and savings. Identify your requirements and desires, and develop the skill to effectively prioritize between them. Your preferences are the aspirations that you possess but can relinquish. Those are the initial steps that should be prioritized when contemplating reducing expenses. This section entails the instructions for acquiring knowledge on the concepts of saving and subsequently making investments. Establish objectives for your forthcoming endeavors and acquire the skills to accumulate financial resources towards their attainment. It is more convenient and effective to engage in tasks with a clearly defined objective.

When devising your aspirations, acquaint yourself with both short-term and long-term objectives. This constitutes the fundamental essence of budgeting.

Herein, we present an illustration of each expenditure as a reference. However, it is important to note that individual circumstances may vary, and what one person perceives as a necessity, another might consider a luxury.

Requirements: accommodations, transportation, utilities, and groceries

Allocation of financial resources; contributions to retirement funds, settlement of debts, various modes of savings

Desires/Preferences; subscription-based television services, online media consumption, self-care products, discretionary purchases

Note:

The expense tracker spreadsheet or the PDF document that you have been utilizing serves as an ideal starting point for classifying your expenses based on their distinction as essential or discretionary.

Clearly, a budget would serve no purpose unless one aspires to reduce superfluous expenses. If you do not reduce your expenditure, all your financial transactions will simply become additional entries in a monthly tracking system. Therefore, it is advisable to begin by reducing one's desires. However, it is advisable not to eliminate all expenditures, as it is crucial to allocate a portion of your resources for leisure activities. Failure to do so may lead to a complete loss of motivation and discouragement during difficult times. Nevertheless, it is imperative to allot funds for recreational activities.

Once you have successfully reduced your desires, your subsequent task entails determining strategies to economize on your necessities. One method to prevent the risk of causing significant errors in financial management is to establish strict guidelines determining the proportion of income allocated to various expenditure categories.

To provide contextual insight, let us delve into a series of budgeting principles that can be adhered to in order to enhance one's quality of life.

Budgeting Rules

Rule #1: 25%

To begin, kindly review your expenditure table provided above and proceed to classify each item into four distinct categories. This process entails ensuring that all of your expenses are appropriately assigned to one of the following categories: taxes, living expenses, debts (excluding mortgage payments), and housing (which includes mortgage and/or rent).

Apportion one quarter of your earnings towards taxation. Dedicate a portion equating 25% of your income to the payment of taxes. Assign a percentage equivalent to the first quarter of your earnings for tax purposes.

Indeed, it is evident that one's taxes are deducted prior to the actual receipt of their income. Conduct an estimation of the monetary amount allocated for taxation. Allocate a quarter of your pre-tax income towards these expenses, considering both the various and federal assessments.

Dedicate a further 25% of your earnings towards housing.

Regardless of whether you are a homeowner or a tenant, it is imperative to ensure that your expenditure on housing does not exceed 25% of your monthly income before taxes are deducted. This indicates that regardless of your income level, it is advisable for your monthly mortgage or rent payments to constitute no more than 25% of your total earnings.

Designate an additional 25 percent of your pre-tax earnings towards debt payments.

Establish a maximum threshold of 25% for all loan payments. This excludes mortgage repayments. Please be advised that as your debt obligations approach 30% of your pretax income, the probability of encountering difficulties in obtaining credit increases.

Ultimately, it is advisable to apportion a quarter of your income before taxes towards covering your living expenditures.

This is the place where you allocate all remaining resources. Your savings ought to be stored within that receptacle, including provisions such as food and groceries.

Recommendation: By effectively reducing expenses in every category, it will be evident that a surplus amount can be allocated towards savings, investments, and fortifying one's contingency fund. This is the sole method by which you can cease the cycle of relying on each paycheck for sustenance. For example, it is important to ensure that your contingency fund comprises an amount equivalent to your monthly living expenses for a period of 3-6 months.

Please take note of the importance of diligently monitoring all aspects if you aspire to achieve success and gain insight into your spending habits.

Second Rule: The 50-30-20 Budgeting Rule

This is undoubtedly the singular principle that will enable you to acquire proficiency in classifying your desires and necessities. Could you please explain the manner in which it facilitates the achievement of that specific task? Now, let us examine its functionality to facilitate your comprehension of how it can truly facilitate a transformative journey in your life.

In this regulation, the process entails the division of one's income after taxation, also referred to as net pay, into three overarching categories, followed by the allocation of respective portions as outlined below:

Devote half of your net earnings to necessary expenditures.

This encompasses anything that is indispensable or impossible to eschew on a monthly basis. It encompasses expenditures such as vehicle loans, real estate mortgages, credit card bills, rental payments, and grocery purchases, among others. In a general sense, this category ought to encompass expenditures such as accommodation, groceries, utilities, and transportation.

Devote 30% of your net earnings to discretionary expenses or personal preferences.

These are discretionary expenditures of a personal nature, which you may consider relinquishing if desired, such as cable television subscriptions, charitable contributions, mobile phone plans, fitness center memberships, personal grooming expenses, recreational activities, retail purchases, dining out, pet-related costs, childcare services, internet usage, and so forth.

Advice: In the event that you have already attended to the remaining classifications of expenditures, there is no cause for concern. However, if you possess a strong determination, you can reduce this. If an expenditure falls within the confines of your allocated 30%, you are exhibiting responsible spending behavior! Developing a budget specifically for this purpose can serve as a source of motivation, as it provides you with a predefined allowance for indulgence.

Devote a portion amounting to 20% of your net earnings to debt repayment and savings.

This category is for helping you to pay up your outstanding debts as you also contribute towards a retirement fund, your emergency fund etc.

In order to provide you with a more comprehensive understanding, allow me to provide an illustrative example that will offer a clearer perspective on this matter.

Introducing John, a recent entrant in the workforce, whose salary amounts to $2,250. He is responsible for covering his student loans, yet he demonstrates an adept ability to simultaneously effectively handle the payments while also making contributions towards a Roth IRA and comfortably meeting his financial obligations.

Annual income: $36000

Net Income (factoring in an assumed 25% deduction for taxes and 401k contributions): $2250

Needs/Essentials 49%

Transportation; $75

Housing; $750

Utilities; $75

Groceries; $200

The sum amounts to $1,100, representing approximately 49% of the overall net income.

Debt and Saving 21%

Retirement contributions; $225

Emergency funds; $200

Car debt; $50

The aggregate sum amounts to $475, representing a proportion of 21% relative to the net income.

Lifestyle choices 30%

The cumulative sum amounts to a total of 675, representing 30% of the net income.

Certainly, it is evident that your expenditures will vary in comparison to those of others. What holds significance is the vigilant observation of your proportions, thereby ensuring that you do not find yourself in a state of economic hardship. Indeed, it is possible to reduce expenditures in certain domains while allocating additional resources to others. As an example, it is possible to curtail your lifestyle expenditures by 20% while concurrently augmenting your debt repayment and savings allotment to 30%. Any approach that suits your needs and preferences is acceptable. However, it is crucial to bear in mind that your lifestyle choices must never surpass a threshold of 30%. All other elements may fluctuate, but only your lifestyle choices can invariably decline. If you possess a true determination to revolutionize your life, it is possible to endure without these desires.

Please take note that your retirement contributions are excluded from the calculation as they are not included in your net pay. This implies that your actual allocation towards debt repayment and savings surpasses what is reflected in the breakdown. Nevertheless, it is advisable to retain the current state; your retirement funds must not be considered in your present financial considerations. When something is not visible, it tends to be forgotten.

If you desire to ascertain whether you are adhering to the 50-30-20 principle, you may utilize Learn Vest as a facilitative tool for accomplishing this task effortlessly.

Avoiding Errors Of Passivity In The Online Environment

According to a statistical report, approximately 90 percent of entrepreneurs experience failure in attaining their income objectives. Either they are unable to adhere to the fundamental principles, or they lack the appropriate level of concentration and commitment required to attain the objectives. Moreover, they are frequently committing significant errors.

It is apparent that they are committing an error that is accountable for the lack of success. If one possesses prior knowledge of commonplace errors, they will have the ability to overcome resulting complications. Nevertheless, prior to embarking on a business endeavor, it will be necessary for you to conduct thorough research and diligently analyze the errors made by others.

In this context, you will be presented with additional information pertaining to the creation of passive income through online means. Furthermore, the prevalent instances of failure and the errors accountable for such outcomes will also be thoroughly examined. If one adheres to the guideline, refrains from typical errors, and maintains concentration, they will be able to achieve financial proficiency and attain easy success in due course.

Critical Errors to Be Avoided at all Costs When Generating Passive Online Income

If you make an erroneous decision, it can indeed yield profound consequences beyond your initial anticipation. Hence, it is imperative that you diligently rectify and surmount the errors in due course.

If you are currently making any errors, it is imperative to exercise caution when revisiting them for the purpose of rectification. It is imperative to refrain from committing these errors in generating passive income online in order to unlock its full potential. Let's explore:

1. Avoid diverting your attention to multiple matters simultaneously. 2. Refrain from placing excessive emphasis on numerous tasks simultaneously. 3. It is advisable not to excessively allocate your attention to multiple objectives. 4. Steer clear of spreading your focus across too many endeavors concurrently. 5. It is inadvisable to overwhelm oneself by attempting to deal with a multitude of matters simultaneously.

To begin with, it is imperative that you refrain from engaging in excessive activities. It is essential to direct your attention towards something that you had initially set your mind upon. Lacking proper attention, you will ultimately find yourself disoriented and financially devoid.

Therefore, it is imperative that you maintain a focused and determined mindset while keeping your attention directed towards a specific and familiar objective. Otherwise, the outcome will be a significant failure. If one lacks focus, it would be advisable to return to the task, diligently conduct thorough research, and upon completion, one will soon have the opportunity to optimize the advantages.

2 Explore the misalignment

Frequently, even the experts overlook this aspect. They frequently neglect to investigate the discrepancy and implement the required adjustments. If you do not perceive these minor, trivial deviations as a matter of concern, it is essential to recognize their potential to pose significant risks and detriment to both you and your business endeavor.

It is imperative to consistently observe and analyze the system while seeking a comprehensive understanding of its structure and functioning. Without a comprehensive overview, one would be unable to identify the deficiencies or effectively prioritize organizing tasks. After identifying and rectifying the misalignment, you will be well-prepared and safeguarded.

3 Follow up

Ultimately, it is imperative that you refrain from making the same error repeatedly, as it is beyond your means to do so. Failure to adhere to a subsequent course of action can pose significant risks and potentially result in the unfortunate consequence of losing one's business. Consequently, it is imperative to maintain concentration and consistently pursue tasks.

There may exist numerous matters requiring attentiveness, yet it is imperative for one to acquire knowledge of the paramount ones and prioritize accordingly. After acquiring the necessary skills for your role, the remaining tasks will become effortless and seamlessly integrated into your routine.

Acquire Knowledge On Unlocking Passive Income Strategies That Have The Potential To Transform Your Future

If one were to inquire of a group of one hundred individuals whether they possess a genuine desire to augment their financial prosperity, it is highly probable that the response from each and every participant would be in the affirmative. When inquiring about their level of commitment, approximately fifty percent of individuals will simply shrug in response. In truth, the majority of individuals do not exhibit genuine dedication or concern towards their personal well-being, let alone their financial prosperity. However, it is those individuals who truly demonstrate unwavering commitment to taking decisive measures that ultimately bring about meaningful changes in their own lives.

The primary distinction between individuals of high socioeconomic status and those in low socioeconomic conditions lies in their propensity for decisive action, as wealthy individuals exhibit a strong commitment to their financial well-being, while the financially disadvantaged tend to contemplate change without frequently undertaking the necessary actions to actualize it.

If you possess a genuine desire to enhance your financial prosperity, it is prudent that you peruse this article, for it serves as the nascent stage - the juncture at which matters take a decidedly solemn turn and transformative shifts commence.

Are you firmly dedicated to this cause? Given that you are still perusing the content, it can be inferred that you are. Alright, let's delve into the crux of the matter.

A large number of individuals are acquainted with the term 'passive income', yet a large majority lack a complete comprehension of its concept. Passive income is characterized as income that does not necessitate active labor. Put simply, even while enjoying a sunny beach getaway with your family, it is still possible to generate income. The crux of consistently generating and increasing wealth lies in acquiring passive income rather than relying solely on active income.

For instance, in the professions of a medical practitioner, legal counsel, server in the food and beverage industry, or astronaut, once the cessation of work occurs, no monetary compensation is earned. Your operational revenue has been depleted. Despite having an abundance of financial resources, one cannot augment their wealth unless they don appropriate work attire, traverse to their destination, and engage in productive labor.

Affluent individuals often prioritize the accumulation of passive revenue as a means to augment their wealth on a daily basis, irrespective of whether they engage in professional pursuits or leisurely activities. This is the reason why the affluent continue to accumulate wealth while the rest of society experiences a decline in financial well-being. And poorer. And poorer.

Fair warning. Do not presume that the establishment of passive income is a task devoid of challenges; quite the contrary. It requires effort to establish a solid foundation, and it necessitates careful strategizing and dedication to construct that foundation. Without building this foundation, the attainment of passive income remains unattainable.

Let us consider an alternative perspective: you have the option of dedicating 40 hours this week towards employment as an office clerk in an insurance company, which would yield a remuneration of merely $10 or $12 per hour. However, dedicating 40 hours to the establishment of your passive income can provide you with a consistent flow of earnings at a rate of $10 or $12 per hour (or even higher), maintained continuously throughout the day, including weekends.

Consider the prospect of making $400 prior to awakening in the morning. Envision the potential of acquiring a sum of $50 while you partake in your morning meal. Consider the scenario of embarking on a week-long vacation and upon return, discovering a check amounting to $2000 within the mail. That's passive income.

How can you achieve this objective? Firstly, it is advisable to refrain from resigning from your current employment, as significant effort will be necessary before you can sustain yourself solely through passive income and discontinue your conventional work schedule. Developing a sustainable source of income requires adopting a long-term perspective, focusing on the future rather than immediate gains. Therefore, it is crucial to ensure the timely payment of your expenses during this interim period. However, it is important to bear in mind that the affluent individuals are those who proactively engage in action. The indigent are those individuals who return from their occupation and "power down."

Real estate has proven to be a highly effective means of generating passive income. For instance, if you were to acquire an exquisite property or commercial establishment and subsequently lease it, while your mortgage installments remain lower than the rental income generated, you would effectively generate passive income.

The significant predicament lies in the fact that the majority of individuals lack the substantial financial resources necessary to acquire real estate. Consequently, it may become necessary for you to adjust your ambitions slightly in order to generate more modest levels of passive income, employing a significantly smaller initial investment. This approach will allow you to gradually progress towards real estate investment in due course.

Multi-level marketing, abbreviated as MLM, has consistently served as a means of generating passive income for individuals who lack substantial initial investment. Although there are those who tend to avoid MLM systems, it is imperative to grasp the fundamental disparity between their operational methods and the portrayal presented in infomercials before entering into such endeavors.

In order to generate substantial income in an MLM system, it is imperative to dedicate diligent effort rather than expecting instant monetary gains upon joining. If you are acquainted with individuals who have achieved notable success in any MLM enterprise, it is highly likely that they have devoted extensive periods of time and effort towards sales activities. This presents a significant drawback, as the majority of individuals are averse to engaging in sales activities. The most effective approach to generate passive income entails the identification of a legitimate business opportunity that does not necessitate any sales efforts.

Position Yourself for Optimal Achievement

To achieve financial success, it is imperative to ensure the absence of any outstanding debts and uphold a state of organization. I express the aspiration that my readers acquire the competence to independently manage their individual financial situations. Therefore, this chapter aims to assist readers in effectively managing their debts and enhancing their personal financial organization.

Managing Debt

Debt is unforgiving. If you consistently meet all of your obligatory payments in a punctual manner, it is unlikely that debt plagues you. Nevertheless, in the event that you are falling behind on payments or experiencing difficulty in meeting them, it is imperative that you adhere to the guidelines provided in this section for efficacious debt management.

Effectively handling financial obligations involves the discerning allocation of resources. Typically, it is advisable to give precedence to the repayment of the debt that accrues the highest interest rates and fees. For instance, if you have equal outstanding balances on two distinct credit cards that have varying interest rates, it is advisable to evaluate which card is incurring a higher cost for you. Given that card 1 carries an interest rate of 20%, whereas card 2 bears an interest rate of 10%, it would be beneficial to prioritize the repayment of card 1 while making only the minimum payment on card 2. According to specialists, the optimal approach to settling outstanding balances on multiple credit cards entails concentrating lump sum payments on a single card at a time. Furthermore, it is essential to never overlook the importance of making a minimum monthly payment, as failure to do so could have dire consequences for your financial well-being.

Alternatively, it is worth considering that prioritizing the repayment of the smallest credit card debt prior to addressing the larger balances could yield psychological advantages. Renowned millionaire David Ramsey, who previously faced financial distress, asserts that he acquired inspiration and drive upon successfully settling even the slightest fraction of his debts. He offers the suggestion that individuals who are confronted with overwhelming emotions regarding their debts initiate the process of attaining financial stability by prioritizing the repayment of any remaining, feasible debts. The outstanding debts will appear relatively less burdensome due to their reduced number, even though the overall amount owed is greater compared to if a single significant debt had been prioritized. Ultimately, the determination of whether the psychological advantage obtained through expeditiously settling a debt is commensurate with the additional interest charges will rest on your decision-making process.

Furthermore, certain delinquent accounts may be transferred to a collections agency. When an organization does not receive the outstanding payment within the period they consider reasonable, they reserve the prerogative to refer that account to an external entity entrusted with the task of procuring the funds on their behalf. Put differently, should you neglect to make timely payments for your financial obligations, there is a possibility that you may become involved in a dispute with a debt collection agency. Regrettably, a failure to remit payment to the collections agency within the specified timeframe, typically sixty days, will have an adverse impact on your credit rating. Hence, it would be advantageous in the long term to settle your accounts not held by a collections agency before allocating substantial payments towards those that have been referred to collections. This measure will serve as a safeguard against the impact of additional outstanding debts on your credit score, over and above the ones presently affecting it.

An alternative approach to managing debt arises through the avenue of a settlement. If you happen to possess an unpaid balance on your credit card, it is conceivable that you may be offered the opportunity to negotiate a settlement with the credit card company at a value lower than the initial balance. While not every company may be inclined to reach a settlement, certain companies will be amenable to accepting a partial payment, thereby waiving the remaining amount, with the intention of discontinuing their collection efforts in order to conserve resources. Please contact your credit card company and request to be connected with a representative who possesses the necessary expertise to engage in negotiations for a debt settlement. The strength of your argument can be bolstered by your willingness to either make a lump sum payment or establish a payment plan of a highly abbreviated duration. Please be advised that the credit card company may opt to terminate your card or reduce your credit limit as a condition of the settlement.

If you are presently confronting the burden of high-interest debts stemming from diverse origins, it would be prudent to contemplate the merits of obtaining a debt consolidation loan. For instance, an individual may have outstanding debts on their various credit card, medical, and utility expenses. Debt consolidation loans are designed to cater to individuals who have financial obligations to multiple institutions.

In accordance with the provisions of said agreement, a financially affluent creditor commits to settling the remaining liabilities of the debtor, thereby affording the debtor a reduction in expenses incurred from future interest accumulation. In return, the debtor remunerates the creditor through consistent monthly installments until the principal amount of the debts, along with the creditor's designated interest rate, is fully repaid. The lender obtains interest from the borrower at a reduced rate compared to the amount that the borrower would have paid to the original entities owed.

Knowledgeable individuals have documented numerous advantageous outcomes resulting from the utilization of debt consolidation loans. Specifically, they achieve a reduction in expenditure on interest. Furthermore, it is commonly observed that a debt consolidation loan tends to diminish the frequency of collection-related phone calls that a debtor encounters. In addition, the credit scores of the debtors will be maintained on the condition that they consistently make punctual payments to the creditor. Among various debt management alternatives, a debt consolidation loan operates by amalgamating all of an individual's unresolved debts into a singular, consolidated debt.

Additionally, bankruptcy presents itself as an alternative approach to effectively handle outstanding debts. In opposition to commonly held misconceptions, it is important to note that a declaration of bankruptcy does not offer legal protection against one's unpaid financial obligations. Instead, when a court bestows upon you the privilege of filing for bankruptcy, you will remain liable to repay the entirety of your outstanding debts. Nevertheless, as you make arrangements to settle your outstanding debts, you will be afforded legal safeguards through the federal judicial systems. Chapter 7 and Chapter 13 are the prevailing forms of bankruptcy petitions, each offering debtors distinct approaches to debt repayment.

In the majority of instances, Chapter 7 bankruptcy petitions necessitate that debtors discharge their outstanding obligations within a period of six months or fewer. Nevertheless, it is not obligatory for them to utilize cash as a means of conducting their transactions. In accordance with the provisions outlined in a Chapter 7 petition, the indebted individual retains the option to dispose of their high-value possessions and assets through sale or liquidation. Subsequently, the funds derived from the sale of said assets are allocated towards settling the outstanding debts owed to the creditors. The judiciary will ascertain the assets that must be liquidated in order to ensure that the debtor's loss of properties aligns with their specific circumstances.

In certain instances, it is possible for you to retain a significant portion, or even the entire corpus, of your estate. Several items are exempt from the purview of Chapter 7 bankruptcy law as dictated by federal regulations. Every state possesses distinct legislation concerning the categories of assets that may be deemed exempt from a Chapter 7 bankruptcy petition. Should you meet the eligibility requirements set by your state, it may come as a surprise to learn that you have the potential to retain full ownership of your assets while simultaneously being granted a bankruptcy.

Conversely, if you receive consistent income, it is probable that you meet the criteria for filing a Chapter 13. If you are able to furnish the courts with substantiating evidence, such as a valid paystub, pertaining to your income, it would be advisable to contemplate initiating a petition for Chapter 13 bankruptcy. Pursuant to the provisions of said agreement, the debtor presents a comprehensive repayment arrangement delineating their proposed strategy for settling their outstanding financial obligations. In the event that the presiding judge determines that the applicant possesses the capacity to adhere to the conditions laid out in their proposal, the debtor shall be granted a Chapter 13 bankruptcy, thereby securing comprehensive safeguarding under federal jurisdiction that prohibits any further undue intrusion by debt collectors.

Financial Organization

It will prove highly advantageous to arrange your financial matters alongside all relevant documentation and files. This meticulousness will greatly assist you in formulating a comprehensive monthly budget, a topic that will be thoroughly addressed in the upcoming chapter. Currently, your primary focus should be directed towards ensuring that all of your documentation is properly organized. Maintaining proper organizational skills is crucial as failure to keep a record of your outstanding bills may result in unforeseen financial penalties, such as accruing interest and incurring late fees. It is not necessarily mandatory to implement every suggestion provided in this section for the purpose of organizing your finances. Nevertheless, I suggest selecting the guidelines that are applicable to your individual circumstances in order to devise a functional framework that proficiently manages your financial matters.

First and foremost, ensure prompt adherence to your financial obligations. Please ensure that you retrieve the items from your mailbox every day. Upon receipt of a bill through postal mail, promptly proceed to unseal and examine its contents. Gazing upon the outstanding balance exhibited on your bill might prove disagreeable, nevertheless, deferring such an encounter shall not render any benefit. Subsequently, should you possess the requisite resources, promptly settle the aforementioned bill. Subsequently, you can mark that bill as completed from your mental or tangible roster of financial obligations and dismiss it from your consideration.

In a similar vein, maintain a record of your expenses by creating a list of bills arranged in three columns. This should not be mistaken for the three-columned budget that will be elaborated on in the subsequent chapter. Please record all anticipated invoices for the respective month in the leftmost column of your bill register. Currently, it is not necessary to be overly concerned about the exact monetary value that you anticipate appearing on the invoice. Instead, focus on listing the specific bills themselves, such as "utilities" or "car insurance," without assigning a specific dollar amount. Subsequently, record the names of the bills as you receive them, including the corresponding dates of receipt and due dates, in the middle column. Ultimately, in the third column, record the name of every invoice promptly following its settlement, alongside the date of remittance. Should you find yourself in a situation where you encounter a dispute with a company or creditor regarding any of your bills, it will be advantageous for you to have the aforementioned list on hand for reference. Moreover, you will not be left with any doubt regarding the necessity of allocating funds for your credit card payment, exemplifying this point.

Furthermore, it is imperative that you maintain a well-arranged assortment of invoices and expenditures. Ensure that you gather all of your bills in one designated location. Maybe you could allocate a designated drawer within a desk, a folder within a file cabinet, or a level within a stacking tray. Regardless, maintaining all of your bills in a single physical location will mitigate the need to frantically search for documentation of a specific bill when it is required. If you opt to receive electronic bills, it is advisable to maintain a consolidated storage system, such as a file folder or email folder, to conveniently organize all your bills. Subdirectories are also acceptable, provided that you have a main directory that encompasses them all. In the same vein, you have the liberty to partition or categorize your tangible bills within their central storage location as well.

If you find technology intriguing, it is worth considering the utilization of professional financial software. Numerous financial software applications are developed with the aim of assisting users in effectively managing their individual financial affairs. Furthermore, the utilization of a basic Microsoft Excel document can assist individuals in maintaining a structured approach towards financial organization.

Furthermore, it is suggested by financial experts that individuals establish two checking accounts as a means to effectively streamline their financial management. They propose the establishment of separate accounts for essential expenditures and non-essential expenses. It is advisable to strive for maintaining a sufficiently high balance in your essential expenditure account to meet all your obligatory expenses for the month. Your secondary account is intended for recreational purposes. As an illustration, in the scenario where you engage in social outings involving the consumption of beverages with acquaintances, maintaining a supplementary account specifically designated for discretionary expenditures would serve the purpose of safeguarding your allocated funds for utility expenses from being inadvertently spent on alcoholic beverages. It is advisable to refrain from removing the debit card associated with your essential expenditure checking account from your place of residence. Certain individuals take the drastic measure of physically dividing the card, retaining solely the numerical information in order to facilitate electronic payment of bills.

If you and a partner, spouse, or family member happen to have a joint account, the importance of maintaining organization becomes even more pronounced. In addition to assuming accountability for your personal expenditures, savings, and financial planning, you are also obliged to monitor the financial affairs of another individual. Should you be unfamiliar with the expenditures made by the individual associated with your account, there is a potential risk of inadvertently causing an overdraft. The individuals who possess joint ownership of an account should engage in regular and ongoing communication pertaining to the financial matters concerning said account. In addition, it is highly recommended that both parties engage in consultation prior to making significant purchases.

Additionally, it is imperative for individuals who have chosen direct deposit as their preferred payment method to consistently verify the prompt and accurate arrival of their paychecks into the designated account. Please ensure to verify the balance of the linked account when anticipating the arrival of your paycheck through direct deposit, in order to avoid inadvertent overspending beyond the available funds. Engaging in such an action may result in the imposition of overdraft fees, even in light of the imminent arrival of your upcoming paycheck. It is a prevailing practice for funds deposited into a bank account to be subjected to a temporary hold until the bank establishes their authenticity. Regularly monitoring your account balance upon receiving your salary can assist in mitigating both financial anxieties and unnecessary expenditure.

Subsequently, upon the establishment of your budget, it is imperative that you consult it prior to undertaking any significant financial decision. Whilst the upcoming chapter details the budget plan with the intention to provide users with monthly financial guidance, it is imperative that you review it at greater frequency than once every thirty days. To maintain organizational efficacy, it is imperative to frequently revise your financial plan and implement any requisite adjustments.

In conclusion, ensure the retention of each and every financial document that comes into your possession. Ensure that they are methodically arranged in a centralized location. Please refrain from disposing of any receipts, pay stubs, bills, I.O.U.s, or any other pertinent documents that demonstrate your expenditure and income.

Are you finding your eBook to be engaging thus far? Please consider subscribing to our complimentary newsletter to receive exclusive discounts, opportunities for book giveaways, and VIP promotions.

When an individual relies on us for their welfare, we are compelled to exercise greater prudence in our financial management, lest that individual becomes resentful or, in a worse scenario, withdrawn from our care.

I was raised in Milwaukee, Wisconsin, and presently, I continue to reside there. I find great joy in residing within the urban landscape due to the incessant and diverse array of activities and events that continuously take place. I share a strong affinity for residing in close proximity to Lake Michigan as well. The scenery remains captivating throughout all four seasons. The individuals in my social circle who are acquainted with my current state perceive me as a self-reliant and autonomous individual. Nonetheless, there was a time when I did not possess these qualities. I had once been financially destitute. In fact, I was formerly without a permanent residence.

Discussing the matter at present is quite challenging; however, I previously struggled with a gambling addiction. I liked the slots. My father is the individual who provided me with instruction in this matter, and it is not unexpected that he experienced financial hardship for a significant portion of his life as well. However, during my adolescence at the age of 16 or 17, he experienced a continuous series of victories. He had been engaged in a game of blackjack and emerged victorious with substantial winnings. That is primarily the impression I have of him: a triumphant individual, accomplished and affluent. He successfully maintained his position of financial stability for approximately four to five years before experiencing another period of insolvency. However, prior to succumbing to complete financial ruin, he imparted upon me the educational knowledge and strategies conducive to gambling. I originally began my gambling endeavors with blackjack;

however, I eventually developed a compulsive attraction towards slot machines.

Upon gaining independence, I managed to sustain my livelihood through engaging in the pursuit of gambling. I experienced a period of personal decline when I began consuming alcohol. The casinos entice individuals, and they provide beverages in order to retain their presence at the gaming tables and slot machines. I became excessively engaged in consuming alcoholic beverages, resulting in an intoxicated state and imprudently squandering all my finances on slot machine games. I would also go way in debt with the house. I would lack the comprehension of the consequences due to my inebriated state. The following day, I would come to the realization of my actions.

After an arduous journey, I ultimately found myself destitute and without shelter. However, it was not until I encountered a companion named Lena, who had also struggled with alcohol addiction, that I discovered the path towards sobriety and successfully rebuilt my life. She facilitated my connection with Alcoholics Anonymous and Gamblers Anonymous. After an extensive period of undergoing rehabilitation, I successfully attained employment, secured a modest studio apartment, and as time has elapsed, it has now been two years. I have finally regained my sense of identity. I feel great. "

www.ingramcontent.com/pod-product-compliance
Lightning Source LLC
Chambersburg PA
CBHW050235120526
44590CB00016B/2091